Applesoft
Carpenter II

Seven Utility Programs
for Applesoft Programmers

Wayne Eastwood

Glen Bredon

Val J. Golding

Produced by:
Brian Wiser & Bill Martens

 Apple PugetSound Program Library Exchange

Applesoft Carpenter II

ACKNOWLEDGEMENTS

Applesoft Carpenter II was programmed by Wayne Eastwood, Glen Bredon, and
Val J. Golding and published by A.P.P.L.E. in 1981. We would like to thank them for
creating so many tools that were beneficial for Apple II users.

The Lister, The Comparer, The Cruncher, The Converter, The Constructer are
copyright © 1981, 1983 by Wayne Eastwood

The Finder is copyright © 1981, 1983 by Glen Bredon

The Keeper is copyright © 1981, 1983 by Val J. Golding

The Cover and Book were designed by Brian Wiser.

PRODUCTION

Brian Wiser   → Cover, Design, Layout, Editing
Bill Martens   → Scanning, Initial Manual, Software Updates

DISCLAIMER

About the Authors

Wayne Eastwood

Wayne Eastwood was an A.P.P.L.E. member and programmer who worked with a number of the early Apple II programmers. He was a an original co-producer and programmer for *Applesoft Carpenter II*. He was also an author for *Nibble* magazine, having written *The Stepper*, a debugger for the Apple II.

Val J. Golding

Val J. Golding founded Apple Pugetsound Program Library Exchange (A.P.P.L.E.) in 1978 with the help of Mike Thyng and Bob Huelsdonk at the suggestion of Max Cook, a manager at the ComputerLand where Val bought his Apple II.

Val also wrote for *Softdisk*, *On-three* and other technology magazines over the years primarily making his mark in the early years of Apple computing.

As the founder, Val was instrumental in guiding the company to the position it is in now. Val was the Managing Editor of *Call-A.P.P.L.E.* magazine and also served as the chairman of the board of directors.

His wife and daughters were a big part of documenting his stories about his hobby of Cable Cars, and he was the editor of a highly acclaimed newsletter for his daughter's school. He passed away at age 77 on July 2, 2008 after a long battle with cancer.

Glen Bredon

Glen E. Bredon was a mathematics professor and computer programmer. He earned his Ph.D. from Harvard University in 1958 and starting teaching at the University of California, Berkeley in 1960. Starting in 1969, he taught at Rutgers University in New Jersey, and eventually retired in 1993.

Glen bought his first Apple II computer in 1979 and began exploring its internal operations because, "I wanted to know more than my students." He programmed and released several best-selling programs for the Apple II computer including: *DOS Master*, *Block Warden*, and *ProSel,* as well as the *Big Mac* and *Merlin* macro assemblers.

The development of *Big Mac* started when Glen found the public domain assembler *TED/ASM* and was dissatisfied in how it worked. He disassembled it, found ways to improve the editor, and added the ability to create macros and shortcuts for coding. He offered his program to A.P.P.L.E. and the user group sold it as *Big Mac* because of its macro capabilities. Val Golding of A.P.P.L.E. later connected Glen with Roger Wagner of Southwestern Data Systems, and that company later sold the assembler as *Merlin*.

A native Californian and concerned environmentalist, Glen spent his summers away from mathematics and computing, preferring the solitude of the Sierra Nevada mountains where he helped establish wilderness reserves. Photography was also one of his passions that he pursued for over 50 years.

Glen passed away May 8, 2000 and left many noteworthy and positive marks on the world with his endeavors.

About the Producers

Brian Wiser

Brian Wiser is a long-time consultant, enthusiast and historian of Apple, the Apple II and Macintosh. Steve Wozniak and Steve Jobs, as well as *Creative Computing, Nibble, InCider,* and *A+* magazines were early influences.

Brian designed, edited, and co-produced many books including: *Nibble Viewpoints: Business Insights From The Computing Revolution, Cyber Jack: The Adventures of Robert Clardy and Synergistic Software, Synergistic Software: The Early Games, The Colossal Computer Cartoon Book: Enhanced Edition, What's Where in the Apple: Enhanced Edition,* and *The WOZPAK: Special Edition* – an important Apple II historical book with Steve Wozniak's restored original, technical handwritten notes.

He passionately preserves and archives all facets of Apple's history, and noteworthy related companies such as Beagle Bros and Applied Engineering, featured on AppleArchives.com. His writing, interviews and books are featured on the technology news site CallApple.org and in *Call-A.P.P.L.E.* magazine that he co-produces. Brian also co-produced the retro iOS game *Structris*.

In 2005, Brian was cast as an extra in Joss Whedon's movie *Serenity*, leading him to being a producer and director for the documentary film *Done The Impossible: The Fans' Tale of Firefly & Serenity*. He brought some of the *Firefly* cast aboard his Browncoat Cruise and recruited several of the *Firefly* cast to appear in a film for charity. Brian speaks about his adventures to large audiences at conventions around the country.

Bill Martens

Bill Martens is a systems engineer specializing in office infrastructures and has been programming since 1976. The DEC PDP 11/40 with ASR-33 Teletypes and CRT's were his first computing platforms with his first forays in the Apple world coming with the Apple II computer.

Influences in Bill's computing life came from *Byte* magazine, *Creative Computing* magazine, and *Call-A.P.P.L.E.* magazine as well as his mentors Samuel Perkins, Don Williams, Joff Morgan, and Mike Christensen.

Bill is a co-producer of many books including *What's Where in the Apple: Enhanced Edition, The WOZPAK: Special Edition, Nibble Viewpoints: Business Insights From The Computing Revolution,* and co-programmer for the iOS version of the retro game *Structris.* He has written many articles which have appeared in user group newsletters and magazines such as *Call-A.P.P.L.E.*.

Bill worked for Apple Pugetsound Program Library Exchange (A.P.P.L.E.) under Val Golding and Dick Hubert as a data manager and programmer in the 1980s, and is the current president of the A.P.P.L.E. user group established in 1978. He reorganized A.P.P.L.E. and restarted *Call-A.P.P.L.E.* magazine in 2002. He is the production editor for the A.P.P.L.E. website CallApple.org, writes science fiction novels in his spare time, and is a retired semi-pro football player.

CONTENTS

1 – Introduction

5 – The COMPARER II v2.2

6 – The LISTER II v2.1

7 – The CRUNCHER II v2.1

8 – The CONVERTER II v2.1

9 – The CONSTRUCTER v1.1

10 – The FINDER

11 – The Keeper

INTRODUCTION

1. Introduction

The Applesoft Carpenter is a collection of seven utilities designed to enhance the productivity of the Applesoft programmer.

2. Hardware Requirements

The Applesoft Carpenter II requires an Apple II, Apple II Plus, or Apple IIe with a minimum of 32K memory. In addition, the Applesoft language must be present in ROM (Apple II Plus, Apple IIe), or in a Language Card.

3. Programs on the Disk

The following is a list of programs on the disk, and a word or two on what they do:

THE LISTER II THE LISTER II.32	Provides a "formatted" listing of Applesoft programs.
THE COMPARER II THE COMPARER II.32	Compares two Applesoft programs and prints a list of the differences (for maintaining control of updates).
THE CRUNCHER II THE CRUNCHER II.32 THE CRUNCHER II.LG	Compacts Applesoft programs to provide quicker loads and faster execution, as well as conserve disk space.
THE CONVERTER II	Converts Integer BASIC files to Applesoft.
THE CONSTRUCTER	Allows Integer BASIC programs to be converted to Applesoft format verbatim to provide backup documentation on what the program originally looked like.

THE FINDER   Allows you to find all occurrences of a
                              given string within an Applesoft program.

THE KEEPER   Aallows you to preserve your Applesoft
                              variables during line editing.

Programs with names with the suffix ".32" are alternate versions for
Apple II computers with 32K memory.

The CRUNCHER.LG is a special version of the CRUNCHER for
working with extremely large programs. This will be discussed in
greater detail in the section on the CRUNCHER.

4. Overview of Common Features

    a.   There is no limit to program file size. The *Carpenter* expects
all programs to be on disk (see Lister II). If a program is too
large for the buffer space allocated, its file is read by sections
until completed.

    b.   At the completion of a run, program statistics (i.e., byte length
and number of lines) are displayed. Note: in some programs,
the byte length data is taken directly from the DOS file header.
In some cases this data is in error by two bytes. No problem
with program action is incurred.

    c.   Some program parameters are set up as variables to allow easy
program customization by the user.

    d.   Data entry modes use all of the Apple II editing features.

    e.   Ctrl-C will exit any of the programs in the *Applesoft Carpenter*
at any point where user input is being requested, or when
information is being sent to the screen or printer.

    f.   All programs are run initially by a BRUN. As long as memory
is not disturbed, programs may be re-run by entering &
RETURN.

g. All error handling is via DOS. On exit, all DOS buffers are freed. Only on a RESET should the user have to issue a CLOSE.

h. Printer modes make use of form-feed to format output to top-of-page.

i. Default values appear on screen under a flashing cursor. An empty RETURN (pressing the RETURN key alone) will accept the default.

THE COMPARER II

VERSION 2.2

The Comparer II compares two standard Applesoft programs both of which are resident on disk. This is excellent for comparing revisions, and documenting changes, especially when more than one programmer is working on a project.

5.1. Program Files

The following files for the COMPARER II are provided on the disk:

THE COMPARER II   for Apples with 48K memory or more, use this program by typing: BRUN THE COMPARER II, or by selecting item 2 from the menu.

THE COMPARER II.32   For Apples with 32K memory, use this program by typing: BRUN THE COMPARER II.32

5.2. Prompts

Printer Slot/Call: Entering a number from 1-7 assigns output to the corresponding slot. A number greater than 7 will be treated as an address to which output will be set. Entering a 0 or pressing RETURN directs output to the screen.

Printer Setup: If output is directed to a printer, an optional setup string is requested. An empty RETURN cancels this option. ESCape is represented on the screen by a flashing "E", control characters by inverse letters. Since cursor control is not available for this string, editing is done by pressing Ctrl-X, which cancels the line and allows reentry of the setup string. The maximum length of the setup string is 35 characters.

Display Width: Width defaults to 40 unless output is directed to a printer. The default width for printers is 80. Entering an empty RETURN accepts the default. Any number from 30 to 132 may be entered. Due to printer output considerations, the actual width is two less than the specified width.

Today's Date: Although designed for dating of comparison runs, any data sting of up to 20 characters may be entered.

Starting Line: Should you desire to compare part of a program rather than the entire program, the starting line number may be entered here.

Ending Line: RETURN instructs *The Comparer II* to start at the first line of your program. The range specified is for line numbers in the ORIGINAL program.

RETURN instructs *The Comparer II* to stop at the last line in the program.

5.3. Operational Considerations

The Comparer II will accept programs on separate disks, so the user is prompted to insert the disk containing the ORIGINAL program. When the file is located, the user is then asked to specify the name of the CURRENT file. If a drive and/or slot was specified in the ORIGINAL file name, it becomes the default value for the CURRENT file.

If the same drive and slot are specified for both files, the user will be asked if both programs are on the same disk. Any entry but "N" assumes a "yes" response. If the response is N, the user will be asked to insert the disk containing the CURRENT file. This disk swapping may take place more than once during a run depending on the size of the programs.

If a range of lines is specified, the information is included in the page header during the run. Since neither program will be scanned completely, no program statistics will be printed.

5.4. Customizing Data

Location	Valid Settings
$0B05 - lower case flag:	$00 for upper case only display
	$20 for upper/lower case display
$0B74 - screen width default:	$26 (decimal 38, WIDTH - 2)
$0BC3 - printer setup string:	$4E (decimal 78)

To resave program, type:

```
BSAVE COMPARER II, A$805, L$1311
```
(Parameters are identical for 32K configuration)

5.5. Program Data

ORIGINAL file buffer: $2000

CURRENT file buffer: $5800 ($3800 for 32K version)

File buffer size: $3700 ($1700 for 32K version)

THE LISTER II

VERSION 2.1

With *The Lister II*, the user has the option of listing a program currently in memory or one that resides on disk. If the program file is on disk, The Lister II functions properly regardless of program size.

6.1. Program Files

THE LISTER II   For Apples with 48K memory or more, use this program by typing: BRUN THE LISTER II, or by selecting menu item 1.

THE LISTER II.32   For Apples with 32K memory, use this program by typing: BRUN THE LISTER II.32

6.2. Default Parameters

When first BRUN, *Lister II* will load a parameter file from disk. If desired, any of the parameters may be changed. * indicates actual width is two less than specified width:

Parameter	Default	Minimum	Maximum
Starting Line Number	0	0	65535
Ending Line Number	65535	0	65535
Left Margin	1	1	48
Screen Width*	40	22	132
Printer Width*	80	22	132
Skips Between Lines	1	0	254
Skips Between Statements	0	0	254
Lines per Page	66	11	254

If any parameter is altered, the user will be given the option of saving the new list as the permanent parameter file. If the program is run by typing & RETURN, the current parameter table is maintained. The user thus has great flexibility in creating both permanent and temporary listing parameters.

NOTE: To avoid printer page breaks, enter 255 as the lines per page parameter.

6.3. Prompts

Once the parameter file is set up, the user will be asked whether to direct output to the screen or to the printer. Specifying 0 will send output to the screen. Specifying a number 1 through 7 will send output to the peripheral in the slot specified (please be sure there is a printer interface card in the specified slot). Specifying any number greater than 7 will cause a machine language printer driver at the address specified to be called each time a character is to be sent to the printer.

The user will then be asked to select Disk or Memory mode. If Disk is selected, the user will be asked to specify a file name. In Memory mode, a program file which has bumped into the program space used by *The Lister II* will cause an error message. The name displayed in *The Lister II's* header is the file name for Disk mode and "CURRENT WORKFILE" for Memory mode.

6.4. Indentation in *The Lister II*

FOR-NEXT loops cause some problems when attempting a formatted listing. Applesoft requires that any NEXT have a FOR, but a FOR may have many NEXTs. Take the following unstructured but convenient example:

```
100  FOR I = 1 TO 10
110  IF A(I)< MIN THEN NEXT : GOTO 200
120  IF A(I)=120 THEN PRINT "."
130  NEXT
200  ...
```

These are not suited to a structured listing. In order to accommodate the widest range of programming styles, the following compromises were effected:

a. For normal FOR-NEXT entry, global indentation takes place as follows:

```
100  FOR X = 1 TO 5
110      PRINT X * 2, X / 2
120  NEXT
```

If more than one NEXT occurs for a FOR at this level, LISTER II will not format the listing correctly.

```
100  FOR A = 1 TO 100
110      FOR X = 1 TO 5 (second FOR statement)
120          IF X < 3 THEN
                 GOTO 150
130          PRINT X * A
140      NEXT X: (NEXT statement)
         GOTO 180
150      PRINT x I A
160  NEXT X (alternate NEXT statement)
170  NEXT A
180 ...
```

b. If the entire FOR-NEXT loop occurs within an IF statement, global indentation takes place as follows:

```
110  IF Y THEN
         FOR X = 1 TO 1000:
             PRINT X:
         NEXT X
120  GOTO 110
```

c. If only the FOR statement appears within an IF statement, only
    local indentation takes place:

```
100   FOR X = 1 TO 10 STEP 10
110      IF FLAG THEN
             FOR X = 1 TO 10 STEP 5
120      PRINT X
130   NEXT X
```

d. If only the NEXT statement appears within an IF statement, global
    indentation takes place:

```
100   INPUT I$
110   FOR X = 1 TO MAX
120      IF A$(X) = "" THEN
         NEXT:
         PRINT "ERROR":
         STOP
130   LET A$(X) = I$(X)
```

6.5. Customizing Data

$8328 lower case flag: $00 for upper case only display
($4328 for 32K version) $20 for upper/lower case display

$815D ($415D) "CURRENT WORKFILE" title: $10 characters max
($415D for 32K version)

To resave program, type:

```
BSAVE THE LISTER II, A$8000, L$1104
```
(A$4000 for 32K version)

6.6. Program Data

File Buffer- $0801
Buffer Length- $7000 ($3000 for 32K)

THE CRUNCHER II

VERSION 2.1

The Cruncher II will "crunch" statements within an Applesoft program to produce more compact, faster code. The crunched file is automatically saved to disk.

7.1. Program Files

THE CRUNCHER II   For Apples with 48K memory or more, use this program by typing: BRUN THE CRUNCHER II, or by selecting menu item 3.

THE CRUNCHER II.32   For Apples with 32K memory, use this program by typing: BRUN THE CRUNCHER II.32

THE CRUNCHER II.LG   For extremely large or complex programs, use this program by typing: BRUN THE CRUNCHER II.LG

7.2. Operational Considerations

Normally, the crunched file will have the same file name as the source file with ".CR" appended. A file name longer than 27 characters will have some final characters deleted to make room. If a file with the new name is already present on disk, the user will be asked if it is to be erased. Any response other than "Y" will exit the program.

The Cruncher II must make three passes of the disk:

1. Pass one finds line references and determines reference status.
2. Pass two performs the actual "crunch" of the program.
3. Pass three writes the "crunched" file out to disk.

7.3. How to Answer the Prompts

There are four possible file types which *Cruncher II* can prepare. The default type removes all REMarks and crunches to a maximum line length of 230 characters by placing multiple statements on a single line. It is designated by the ".CR" suffix. Should the user desire to retain REMark statements, the file suffix becomes ".RR". This option is prompted by the program with "RETAIN REMARKS (Y/N)?". A "Y" input selects this option.

The user also has control of the maximum line length the *Cruncher II* will prepare. With a default (and maximum) value of 230, line length may be reduced to a minimum of 50. This will be of some use to those using Basic line editors. If any value other than 230 is selected, the file suffix becomes ".CS" or ".RS" depending on the REMark option selected. The *Cruncher II* cannot UN-crunch a program. Lines longer than the line length selected will not be reduced in length.

If the option to retain REMarks is not selected, the *Cruncher II* makes every attempt to remove REMark statements. However, when a line containing only a REMark statement is referenced by another statement and the line which follows is also referenced, the REM line must be retained. This line will then contain only the line number and a REM token. A message will be printed on the screen or printer notifying the user.

Three versions are provided: standard versions for 48K and 32K and an LG version for exceptionally complex files with many lines and/or line references.

7.4. Tables Maintained by *The Cruncher II*

While file size is not a problem with *Cruncher II*, two parameters of the file do bear on the size of file that may be crunched. During pass one, two tables are created:

Statbl - Lists each line with its reference status and some additional information. Each line of the source program writes four bytes to this table.

Reftbl - Lists any line which is referenced (by a GOTO, GOSUB, etc.). Each line referenced writes two bytes to this table.

	CRUNCHER II	CRUNCHER II.32	CRUNCHER II.LG
Statbl start	$6000	$4000	$5000
Reftbl start (default)	$8000	$4D00	$7800
Max lines possible	2048	832	2560

7.5. Possible Errors

An attempt by the program to write past the end of Statbl will generate an END OF DATA error. The rare event of an attempt to write past Reftbl will generate an OUT OF MEMORY error. While CRUNCHER II.LG was provided to allow the crunching of exceptionally complex files, both standard versions can have the start of Reftbl relocated by the user.

7.6. Customizing Data

$0AE9 - Lower case flag: $00 for upper case only
$20 for upper/lower case

$0A45-46 Reftbl start: Should not be set below Statbl or above HIMEM adjust upward if an END OF DATA error is encountered, downward if an OUT OF MEMORY error is encountered.

To resave BSAVE THE CRUNCHER II, A$805, L$1554
(Parameters are identical for 32K and .LG versions)

7.7. Program Data

	CRUNCHER II	II.32	II.LG
Input Buffer	$2000	$2000	$2000
Crunched Buffer	$4000	$3000	$3800
Buffer Size	$1F00	$0F00	$1700
Crunched Line Buffer	$0809	$0809	$0809
Raw Input Line Buffer	$091A	$091A	$091A
Start of STATBL	$6000	$4000	$5000
Start of REFTBL	$8000	$4D00	$7800
HIMEM	$9600	$5600	$9600

THE CONVERTER II

VERSION 2.1

The Converter II is a utility designed to automate the conversion of Integer BASIC files to Applesoft. Often, the converted program will run with no modification, but since Integer BASIC has a different syntax from Applesoft, it is wise to check out the converted program thoroughly, even if it appears to work.

8.1. Program Files

THE CONVERTER II   For Apples with 48K memory or more, use this program by typing: BRUN THE CONVERTER II, or by selecting menu item 4.

THE CONVERTER II.32   For Apples with 32K memory, use this program by typing: BRUN THE CONVERTER II.32

8.2. Rules for Conversion

1. Variable names are not truncated to two characters (the maximum number of characters Applesoft pays attention to). Since Applesoft will recognize only the first two, no operational change will be seen between this program and the original *Converter*. Users will still need to modify variables whose first two characters are identical. It was felt however that since the user might not have access to an Integer listing of his or her program, having the whole variable name would aid in completing program conversion. Since these variable names are entered with *The Converter* and not through the Applesoft entry parser, there is no conflict with reserved words; e.g., HGR is a legal variable name in Integer BASIC and will not be considered a token when converted.

2. Major conversion operations include notification flags which send appropriate messages to the user. Messages advise the user as to:

   a. Complicated conversions which might easily be simplified depending on the needs of the user.

   b. Deleted statements which in general have no bearing on program integrity but which might have special significance to some users.

   c. Impossible/unnecessarily complex conversions which have been converted to REMark statements for user handling.

Display of these messages is optional and may be sent to a printer if desired.

The converted program is saved to disk under the Integer file name with ".A" appended. If such a file name exists on the disk, the user will be given the opportunity to exit or erase the file.

If a machine language routine is encountered, conversion stops, the user is notified, and as much of the already converted material as possible is saved.

8.3. Customizing Data

$0DB0 - Lower case flag: $00 – upper case only
                            $20 – upper/lower case

$1743 - Conversion message table start

To resave BSAVE THE CRUNCHER II, A$805, L$1FBC
(Same parameters for the 32K version)

8.4. Program Data

	Converter II	Converter II.32
Output Buffer	$3000	$3000
Input Buffer	$6300	$4300
Buffer Size	$3200	$1200
Applesoft Line Buffer	$900	$900
Integer Line Buffer	$B00	$B00

THE CONSTRUCTER

VERSION 1.1

Since some operations of *The Converter* leave few clues as to what the original Integer program looked like, *The Constructer* was written to provide a literal translation of the Integer program into Applesoft.

9.1. Program Files

THE CONSTRUCTER   For Apples with 48K memory or more, use this program by typing: BRUN THE CON-STRUCTER

THE CONSTRUCTER.32   For Apples with 32K memory, use this program by typing: BRUN THE CON-STRUCTER.32

9.2. Operational Considerations

The new file name will have a ".I" suffix. The new file will act as an Applesoft file when loaded and saved, but it is actually a TEXT file in Applesoft format and will not run. All Integer tokens are brought over into Applesoft as ASCII characters.

Since the constructed file has no Applesoft tokens, The LISTER II will not list the program with absolute precision. The margins will vary slightly due to ASCII spaces which were placed before and after each token conversion.

9.3. Customizing Data

$0DB0 $00 – upper case
          $20 – upper/lower case

To resave BSAVE THE CONSTRUCTER, A$801, L$1514
Same parameters for the 32K version.

9.4. Program Data

	CONSTRUCTER	CONSTRUCTER.32K
Output buffer	$3000	$3000
Input buffer	$6300	$4100
Buffer size	$3200	$1000

THE FINDER

The Finder is a program that will search for, and list all lines in an Applesoft program in which the search string appears.

The search string may be:

- An Applesoft token (keyword)
- A variable
- An ASCII literal
- Any combination of the above

10.1. Operational Considerations

The Finder is installed by typing: BRUN THE FINDER, or by selecting menu item 5. After The Finder is installed, all of its commands are accessed by typing:

& LIST:search string

The search string may be structured as follows:

1. A token or series of tokens. This syntax finds all occurrences of the token or series of tokens, regardless of whether it is a substring reference or complete word. For example:

   & LIST:GOTO   Finds all references to the token GOTO.
   & LIST:GOTO10 Finds all references containing the token
                  GOTO and 10, such as GOTO 10, GOTO 101

2. A token or series of tokens corresponding to the exact target to be found. This is specified by placing a colon (:) after the last character of the target string. For example:

   & LIST:REM: Finds all references to the token REM.
   & LIST:GOTO 10: Finds all occurrences of the string GOTO 10.

23

GOTO 101 is not located using this syntax.

3. A literal string, for example:

`& LIST: "FOR"`   Finds all references to the word FOR. `PRINT "FORWARD MARCH"` would be located, as would `PRINT "THIS PROGRAM IS FOR YOU"`. `FOR I = 1 TO 10` would not be found, as `FOR` is a token in this case, and cannot be specified as a quoted string (or literal).

If you want output directed to a printer, you must issue the appropriate commands from the keyboard (for example, PR#1) before issuing any ampersand commands.

THE KEEPER

The Keeper is a utility written as a shortcut to program
debugging. It preserves the variable table while a program line
is being edited. If you make changes to an Applesoft program
your variable table will normally be destroyed. This can be rather
inconvenient, especially if it takes you a long time to get to the point in
the program where the changes are made.

11.1. Principle of Operation

The principle behind *The Keeper* is simple, but effective: save
the pointers to the variable table in page zero while editing of the
program takes place, then restore them before restarting the Applesoft
program.

11.2. Use of *The Keeper*

To install *The Keeper*, type: BRUN THE KEEPER, or select menu
item 6. This must be done before running your Applesoft program so
The Keeper can set up its buffers.

11.3. Commands

& STEP   This command must be issued before running
                     your Applesoft program. The & STEP
                     command sets up and maintains a buffer
                     area between the end of the program and the
                     beginning of the variable table. The buffer area
                     defaults to 1536 bytes (6 pages), but the size
                     of the buffer may be modified by the user by

entering an optional argument to the & STEP command specifying the number of 256-byte pages to allocate (for example, & STEP 4 allocates four pages of storage).

& SAVE DATA   This command does precisely what its name indicates it might do – it transfers the data in the variable table to the buffer allocated by the & STEP command. This should be done prior to program editing.

& RESTORE DATA   When you are ready to restart your program, enter this command, followed by a GOTO of the line number at which you wish the program to be restarted. It is important to restart the program with a GOTO rather than a RUN, because RUN clears the variable table.

11.4. Limitations

If literal string data is stored within programs (for example: 100 A$ ="HELLO"), and the program is edited while using *The Keeper* commands, the string pointers may no longer point to the correct area of memory. A stop-gap solution would be to insert the following type of code in your program during the development process:

```
100   Z$ = "HELLO"
110   A$ = Z$ + ""
```

Similar situation exists with the DEF FN command. There is no easy solution to this problem, but if the function is defined within the first few program lines, it may remain intact.

www.ingramcontent.com/pod-product-compliance
Lightning Source LLC
Chambersburg PA
CBHW020958180526
45163CB00006B/2411